THE DONNING

by
Colin Handy

Cotswold Walks Between Donnington Brewery Inns

Published
by
Reardon Publishing
PO Box 919, Cheltenham, GL50 9AN,
www.reardon.co.uk
reardon@bigfoot.com

First edition published by
Reardon & Son Copyright 1991

Re-walked and Fully Revised
Reardon Publishing
4th Edition 2012

Written, Researched and Photographed
by
Colin Handy

ISBN: 1-874192-64-2
ISBN (13): 9781874192640

Maps and illustrations
by
Peter T Reardon

This is a truly local guide, written, designed, printed and published
In the Cotswold Area

INTRODUCTION

The Donnington Way

Donnington Brewery brews real ale in the heart of the Cotswolds and maintains 15 inns in arguably the country's ideal location. For many, the name of Donnington means more than good beer; it's a whole way of life.

Now, the pleasure that is Donnington is opened to the rambler in the form of a 62-mile circular walk appropriately called 'The Donnington Way'. You can join the walk at any point in its 15 pub-to-pub sections.

Some Donnington Inns offer bed and breakfast facilities, enabling you to walk distances of your choice. Almost 90% of the walk is in Gloucestershire, although parts of the way pass through Worcestershire, Warwickshire and Oxfordshire. All rights of way listed have been walked to establish their existence on the ground, following wherever possible public footpaths and bridleways.

To help you along the way maps have been drawn for each of the 15 sections but for greater detail consult OS Outdoor Leisure 45 'The Cotswolds' map which covers the entire route.

The Donnington Way is a true Cotswold delight for the rambler who thrives on well-kept countryside and hidden villages. The charm of rural Gloucestershire is treasured by many a walker and the Donnington Way offers an opportunity for that treasure chest to be open to all.

Colin Handy.

THE COUNTRY CODE

Guard against all risk of fire
Fasten all gates
Keep dogs under proper control
Avoid damaging fences, hedges and walls
Keep to paths across farmland
Leave no litter
Safeguard water supplies
Protect wildlife, wild plants and trees
Go carefully on country roads
Respect the life of the countryside

Waymarking colour code:
Blue Arrows = Bridleways
Yellow Arrows = Footpaths only

WHEREVER YOU ROAM IN THE COUNTRY, FOLLOW THE CODE!

The Queen's Head Inn, Stow-on-the-Wold to The Coach and Horses Inn, Longborough (Distance 2¾ miles)

For the convenience of long term parking the walk starts and ends in the Town Square, Stow-on-the-Wold. Stow is regarded as a focal point for the North Cotswolds lying 700 feet above sea level and having eight major routes radiating from its centre. The Town Square is filled with picture postcard houses and shops and remains busy throughout the changing seasons. Prominent among the mellow stone buildings is the starting point of the walk, the Queen's Head, an inn of 'old world' charm.

This, the first of the 15 Donnington public houses, is typical of the style of their inns, retaining as it does a real country pub atmosphere. Tradition is the cornerstone for Donnington's success and the Queen's Head plays its part by offering good food to be enjoyed over traditional pub games.

Leaving the Queen's Head, turn left and head down High Street, passing the old Police Station on your left, and make your way to the busy A429. Turn right and walk out of town on the A road towards Moreton-in-Marsh crossing over after the traffic lights.

After a quarter of a mile, just past the Broadwell turning, there is a layby on your left and an entrance to a house called 'The Paddocks'. Leave the road and start out on a bridleway taking you to Donnington. It was in this pretty little hamlet that the remaining forces of the Royalist troops surrendered to the Parliamentarians on 21 March 1646, which was to be the final defeat of the bitter English Civil War.

At the end of the bridleway, bear right onto an unclassified road. Pass a telephone kiosk on your left and, as the road sweeps right, bear left. After a further 100 yards pick up a footpath sign taking you to Longborough. Soon you pass close to a farm on your right. Go around the barn, turn left, keeping the fence on your left, and go straight ahead over two small fields before once again picking up a bridleway (marked with a blue arrow), taking you into the bottom right-hand corner of the field.

The bridleway, which can get muddy, is well marked and well defined and takes you all the way into the village of Longborough, which is a delight. Keep right and make your way to its green and cross and your first stop, the Coach and Horses.

This compact, cosy inn offers a traditional welcome in a true village style. Its location is such that to look out from the beer garden might well transport you back 100 years. The cross, the cottages and the church lend themselves to be photographed.

The medieval church, with its 13th century tower, is steeped in history and has many interesting features, including gargoyles, burial monuments and a richly sculptured font. It is well worth taking time out to visit.

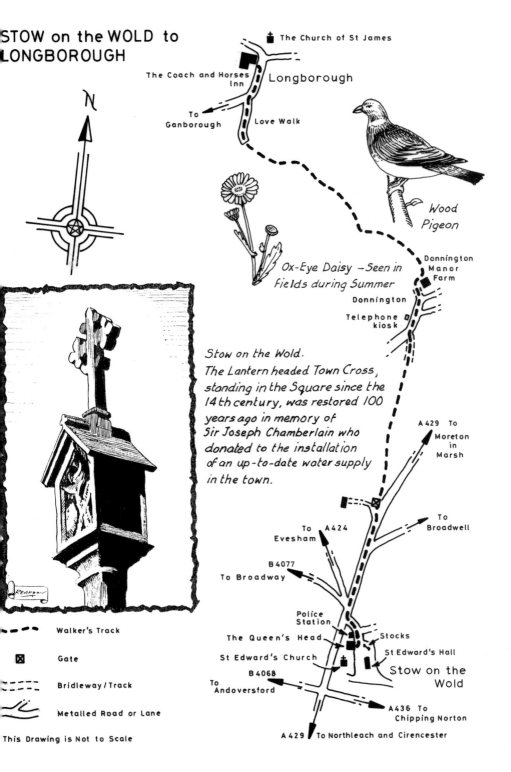

STOW on the WOLD to LONGBOROUGH

The Church of St James

The Coach and Horses Inn

Longborough

N

To Ganborough

Love Walk

Wood Pigeon

Ox-Eye Daisy – Seen in fields during Summer

Donnington Manor Farm

Donnington

Telephone kiosk

Stow on the Wold.
The Lantern headed Town Cross, standing in the Square since the 14th century, was restored 100 years ago in memory of Sir Joseph Chamberlain who donated to the installation of an up-to-date water supply in the town.

A 429 To Moreton in Marsh

To Broadwell

To Evesham   A 424

B 4077

To Broadway

Police Station

The Queen's Head

St Edward's Church

B 4068

To Andoversford

Stocks

St Edward's Hall

Stow on the Wold

A 436 To Chipping Norton

A 429 To Northleach and Cirencester

REARDON

- - - Walker's Track

☒ Gate

- - - Bridleway / Track

～ Metalled Road or Lane

This Drawing is Not to Scale

5

The Coach and Horses Inn, Lonborough
to The Coach and Horses Inn, Ganborough (Distance ¾ mile)

A short steady climb now awaits you as you go from one Coach and Horses directly to another inn of the same name.

As you leave the Longborough Coach and Horses, turn left and climb out of the village towards the A424. Halfway up the hill a memorial bench offers a resting place and a magnificent view over parts of both Warwickshire and Gloucestershire.

Continue the climb to the Y junction and bear left. This short length of road takes you directly to the busy A road. Take care crossing the road and turn left. This is Ganborough. Follow the road for about 200 yards and the second building on your right is the next Coach and Horses inn.

This typical English inn is built entirely of local stone and was originally two cottages and stables. More than 250 years old, the Inn is a popular eating place. It prides itself on its extensive menu and is busy throughout the year.

Water Shrew

LONGBOROUGH to GANBOROUGH

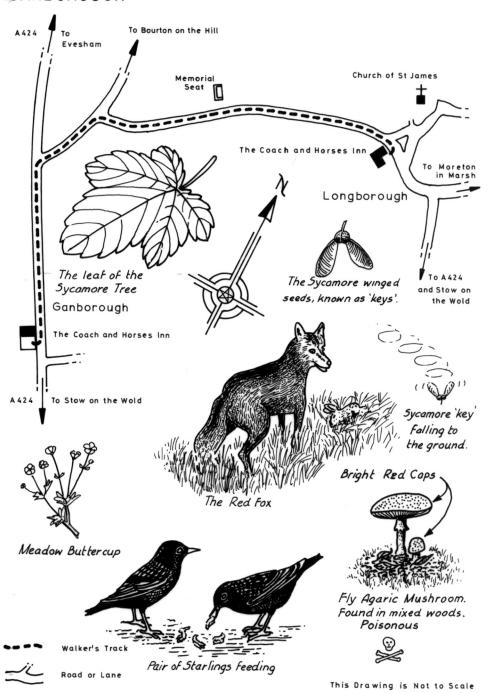

A424
To Evesham

To Bourton on the Hill

Memorial Seat

Church of St James

The Coach and Horses Inn

Longborough

To Moreton in Marsh

N

The leaf of the Sycamore Tree

Ganborough

The Coach and Horses Inn

The Sycamore winged seeds, known as 'keys'.

To A424 and Stow on the Wold

A424
To Stow on the Wold

Sycamore 'key' falling to the ground.

The Red Fox

Bright Red Caps

Meadow Buttercup

Fly Agaric Mushroom. Found in mixed woods. Poisonous

Pair of Starlings feeding

Walker's Track

Road or Lane

This Drawing is Not to Scale

7

The Queens Head, Stow on the Wold

8

The Coach and Horses Inn, Longborough

The Coach and Horses Inn, Ganborough.

The Coach and Horses Inn, Ganborough to The Golden Ball Inn, Lower Swell (via Donnington Brewery)   (Distance 3½ miles)

Leave the Coach and Horses and once again cross the busy A424, turn right and then immediately left down a minor metalled road back to Longborough. You will soon recognise your original point of arrival in the village where you turn right for the bridleway that you left earlier.

At the end of Love Walk and the start of the bridleway, look to your right and you will find a well marked footpath which you follow. After four fields and a copse, with some farm buildings ahead of you, the footpath divides three ways. Take the path going right, through a wooded passage, which takes you back to the A424. Cross straight over onto an unclassified road marked Condicote. Turn left at the first junction marked Upper Swell.

Very soon you arrive at the walk's *raison d'être* – the Donnington Brewery. The mill buildings which house the Brewery have been used in various ways for seven centuries, although they have been converted and rebuilt several times. In 1827 the buildings were bought by the present owners, the Arkell family, who started a brewery here in 1865. The family also farmed the surrounding fields, producing barley for their brewing process. The mill remains in good working order and its wheel can still be used to drive the machinery.

The beautiful Cotswold buildings that form the Brewery stand in an idyllic position, surrounded by lawns and paths which in turn lead to the millpond. Unfortunately, the brewing process does not lend itself to spectators and as a result cannot be thrown open to visitors. However, a fine view is obtained from the minor road as you pass by on your way to the B4077.

At the junction with the B road turn left and carefully walk through Upper Swell. The village boasts a fine Tudor manor house with a two-storey porch alongside a small church, complete with a Norman doorway.

Just before a narrow bridge over the River Dikler, a well marked footpath goes in to the right, taking you across three fields and down a metalled road on the Abbotswood Estate to Lower Swell. The estate boasts a fine 20th century house built by Sir Edwin Lutyens and was once the home of the tractor magnate Harry Ferguson.

As you leave the estate, turn right on the B4068 which takes you directly to your next pub, the Golden Ball, around which, to all intents and purposes, the village of Lower Swell is built.

The Golden Ball offers a wide range of food and beers and a warm welcome. The building dates from the 17th Century and has been licensed for more than 100 years. Again, the Cotswold stone and exposed beams are a delight. A feature of this inn, in the summer months, is the opportunity to watch or join in the traditional garden game of 'Aunt Sally', a game that requires competitors to throw 'sticks' at an 'Aunt Sally' doll to score points.

GANBOROUGH to LOWER SWELL

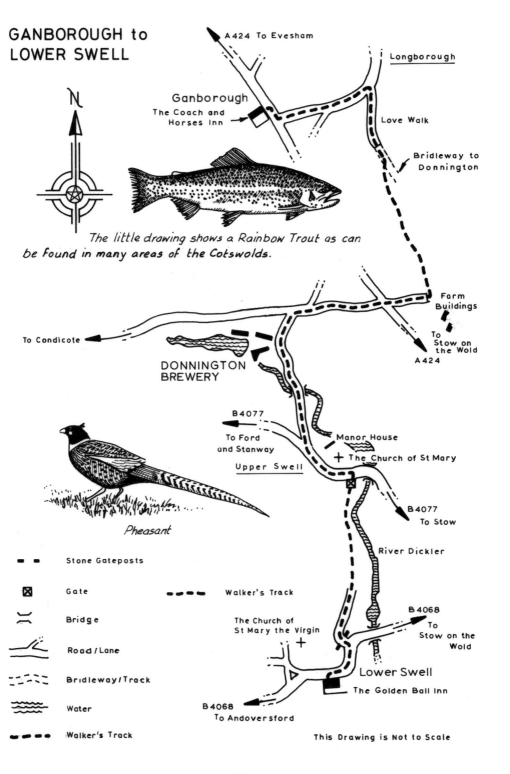

A424 To Evesham

Longborough

Ganborough
The Coach and
Horses Inn

Love Walk

Bridleway to
Donnington

The little drawing shows a Rainbow Trout as can be found in many areas of the Cotswolds.

To Condicote

Farm
Buildings

To
Stow on
the Wold

A424

DONNINGTON
BREWERY

B4077

To Ford
and Stanway

Manor House

✝ The Church of St Mary

Upper Swell

B4077
To Stow

River Dickler

Pheasant

B4068
To
Stow on the
Wold

The Church of
St Mary the Virgin
✝

Lower Swell

The Golden Ball Inn

B4068
To Andoversford

▪▪	Stone Gateposts
⊠	Gate
≃	Bridge
⌇	Road / Lane
⸝⸝⸝	Bridleway / Track
≈≈≈	Water
▬▬▬	Walker's Track

Walker's Track

This Drawing is Not to Scale

11

The Golden Ball Inn, Lower Swell to The Fox Inn, Great Barrington
(Distance 9 miles)

From the Golden Ball turn right onto the B4068 and immediately right again into Rectory Barns. Follow the road as it loops around to the right to rejoin a minor road in the heart of the village. Turn left and walk up the road.

As you leave the village, also leave the road, taking the well marked bridleway on your left. The path leads you over several fields to the attractive Hyde Mill and continues on the bridleway to a metalled service road and the junction of the A424 and the A429.

Taking care, turn right and walk along the A429 towards Cirencester for about 400 yards. Just past the Fosse Manor Hotel, cross over to a layby and follow the footpath sign into the field, heading off at a right angle. The path passes through several fields and a small copse to farm buildings at Heath Hill and continues South for three more fields before it joins an unclassified road where you turn left.

The walk takes you through the pretty village of Wyck Rissington. Continue past the church, with its massive squat Norman tower. After another 200 yards, when the road sweeps left, carry straight on, on a track marked as a 'No Through Road'.

Follow the track for a quarter of a mile where it peters out at the crossing of a bridleway. Turn left and, after a few short steps, turn right to follow a footpath sign taking you straight ahead across the field. In the second field bear slightly left before heading for St. Peter's church at Little Rissington.

The church dates from the 12th Century and is set apart from the present village by a field where the original village lay prior to the Black Death in 1347. An unusual feature of its graveyard is a small 'Military Cemetery' for 75 servicemen who died while stationed at RAF Little Rissington. These include airmen from Canada, Australia, New Zealand and America. The West window of the church is dedicated to their memory and includes a stained glass 'Red Arrow' as a tribute to the squadron which was once stationed here.

From the church, walk up into the village and cross the main road into Pound Lane. The lane loops around left before rejoining the main road at the entrance to Sam's Barn. On your right is a well marked bridleway, which you follow over several fields to Great Rissington. The bridleway is virtually straight the whole way. Ignore turnings to the right and left and continue straight ahead, always keeping the hedge on your right.

At Great Rissington, turn left and follow the main road straight ahead, ignoring a left hand turn. As the main road sweeps left continue straight ahead on the road marked 'Unsuitable for Heavy Goods Vehicles'. Go down the hill and opposite 'Blue Close Cottage' turn left into a small spur road. Turn left again and almost immediately right. The road soon becomes a dirt track. Go straight on for a third of a mile. Just after a large farm barn the track is marked as a bridleway. Keep straight ahead.

LOWER SWELL to
GREAT BARRINGTON

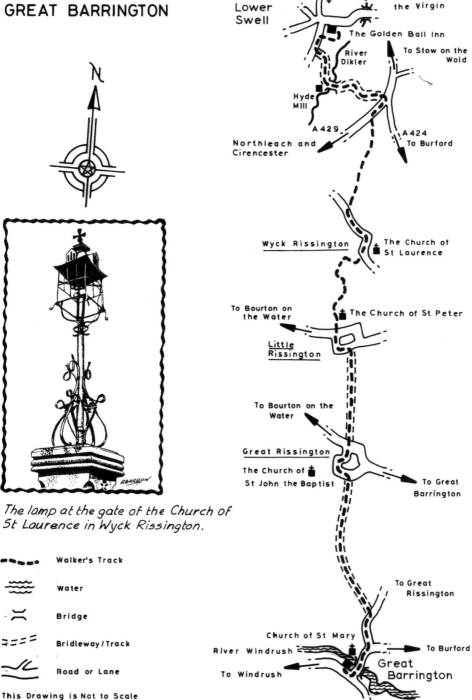

N

Lower Swell

The Church of St Mary the Virgin

The Golden Ball Inn

River Dikler

To Stow on the Wold

Hyde Mill

A 429

Northleach and Cirencester

A 424 To Burford

Wyck Rissington

The Church of St Laurence

To Bourton on the Water

The Church of St Peter

Little Rissington

To Bourton on the Water

Great Rissington

The Church of St John the Baptist

To Great Barrington

To Great Rissington

Church of St Mary

River Windrush

To Burford

Great Barrington

To Windrush

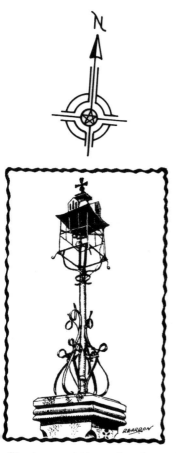

The lamp at the gate of the Church of St Laurence in Wyck Rissington.

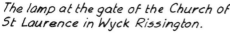

●–●–● Walker's Track

〜〜〜 Water

⌣ Bridge

==== Bridleway / Track

〜〜 Road or Lane

This Drawing is Not to Scale

13

The well used bridleway runs for 1½ miles, dipping into a valley and rising again, before emerging onto the road for Great Barrington, where you turn right. Keep the estate wall of Barrington Park on your right and follow it into the village. Barrington Park contains a grand Palladian style mansion originally built for Earl Talbot.

Pass the village church as you walk by the estate. The church is worth visiting as it boasts many fine features include a delightfully sculptured memorial to Mary Countess Talbot.

Continue down the road to your next port of call, the Fox Inn. In truth, the inn lies equidistant between Great Barrington and Little Barrington alongside the picturesque River Windrush.

The Fox prides itself on being a real English pub in the true sense of the word, unspoilt by time. Visitors can participate in a range of pub games while enjoying good food and beers, or just sit and watch the river as it rushes by.

LITTLE RISSINGTON — GLOUCESTERSHIRE.

Lower Swell

The Golden Ball Inn, Lower Swell.

The Fox Inn, Great Barrington.

The Fox Inn, Great Barrington to The Black Horse Inn, Naunton
(Distance 10¼ miles)

Leave the Fox and take the minor road towards Windrush. After approximately half a mile look for a stone stile in the hedgerow on your right. Climb the stile onto a footpath which runs at a slight left angle straight across the field. Make for the right hand side of the large farm barn ahead of you. Go over another stone stile, keeping the barn and dry stone wall on your left. Cross a small brook and, at the top of the rise, the path divides. Take the path going to your right, cross a farm track and continue straight ahead towards Sherborne. The walk in the Windrush Valley is superb.

As you enter Sherborne between small cottages, you meet a metalled road where you turn right. Follow the road uphill for just over a mile and at the top, where the road sweeps gradually left, look for a footpath sign into a field on your right. Enter the field and turn left onto the footpath.

The path follows the hedgerow to emerge alongside the old stables of Broadmoor Farm and bears left to a metalled road. Turn right and walk through the farm complex. Pass the old farmhouse on your right and after 100 yards turn left onto a footpath taking you down through three fields to the fast flowing River Windrush at New Bridge.

Turn left onto a little used road. After approximately 300 yards, take a well marked bridleway to your right. Keep straight ahead to pass Lower Marsh Farm where you meet a metalled road which becomes easy walking all the way into Bourton-on-the-Water. Look out for a road sign along the lane which points across the fields and gives its distance in 'as the crow flies' miles.

When you meet the major road, turn left and follow the river Windrush through the tourist delights of Bourton-on-the-Water, including its famous Model Village.

The walk through Bourton brings you to the junction with the A429 which you should cross straight over with care. Continue to follow the river on your left using a well used bridleway. The path takes you away from the river and, after two fields, zigzags through a copse. Here, the bridleway splits and you need to continue on the left hand path.

The path soon becomes a road and drops down through an old mill before climbing again. At the T junction turn right and walk through the neat buildings of Aston Farm. The well marked route passes between the farm's enormous sheds and out again into open fields before going into a wood.

Unfortunately, the wooded section can get extremely muddy. Ignore paths going off to the right and keep to the main track to eventually emerge into a fertile valley. It is a magical section full of both wild and domesticated animals.

GREAT BARRINGTON to NAUNTON

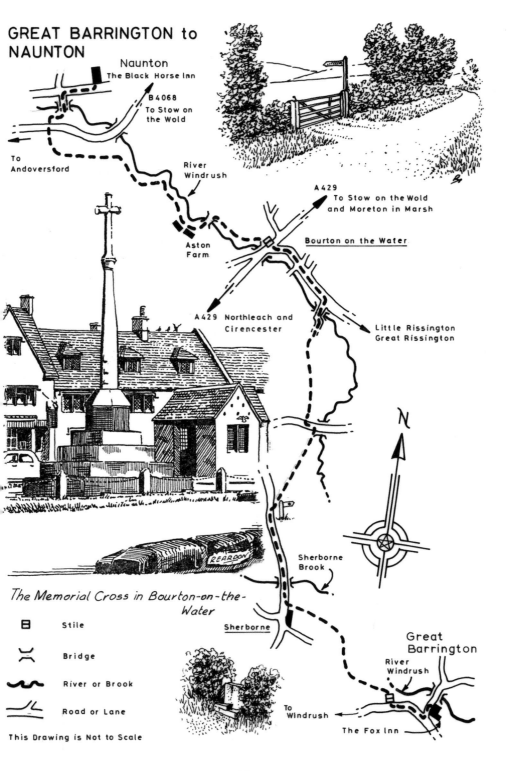

Naunton
The Black Horse Inn

B4068
To Stow on
the Wold

To
Andoversford

River
Windrush

Aston
Farm

A429
To Stow on the Wold
and Moreton in Marsh

Bourton on the Water

A429 Northleach and
Cirencester

Little Rissington
Great Rissington

N

Sherborne
Brook

Sherborne

REARDON

Great
Barrington

River
Windrush

To
Windrush

The Fox Inn

The Memorial Cross in Bourton-on-the-Water

	Stile
	Bridge
	River or Brook
	Road or Lane

This Drawing is Not to Scale

When the footpath meets a metalled road turn left and, after 200 yards of road walking, turn right into another field. Drop down into the valley floor and follow the valley path for a further half mile. Where the path divides, cross the stream on a stone bridge and follow the blue arrowed route up the steep climb at a left angle. At the top of the climb go through a gate and walk straight on through the fairways of the Naunton Downs golf course.

The path soon meets the B4068 road where you turn right. After about 200 yards turn left onto bridleway which drops steeply down to the delightful village of Naunton. Cross the fast flowing River Windrush to emerge onto a metalled road almost opposite your next port of call, the Black Horse Inn.

Built of golden Cotswold stone in the traditional style of the 17th Century, the inn serves good food and beers in peaceful surroundings. The building was originally two cottages which housed farm workers and has beautifully exposed beams to set off its tap room – an inn for a most relaxing rest.

'The Old Mill' viewed from the road bridge in Naunton.

The Black Horse, Naunton

18

The Farmers Arms, Guiting Power.

The Black Horse Inn, Naunton to The Farmer's Arms Inn, Guiting Power (Distance 2 miles)

Prepare yourself for two splendid short sections from Naunton to Guiting Power and on to Kineton. If you had to choose three and a half miles of Gloucestershire to sum up the Cotswolds, these could well be your first choice.

Leave the Black Horse and turn right to make your way through the village, lined with warm limestone houses. You will spot staddle stones and mill wheels and even a dovecote as you climb towards the B4068 and pass St. Andrew's church.

Climb towards the Cheltenham road and just before the top of the hill take a well signed footpath to your right marked 'Wardens' Way'. Follow the yellow arrows. After a short field section, the path joins an unclassified road; turn right and drop down to a T junction.

The footpath to Guiting Power is directly opposite the junction and is well marked. It passes the quiet little wetland that is Guiting Power Nature Reserve before winding its way to emerge to the left of St. Michael's church. A very short road walk takes you into the heart of the village which you will find is almost forgotten by the passing of time.

At the picturesque village green, turn right and make your way to the next stop, the Farmer's Arms. The inn boasts a fine example of an English skittle alley and large function room, both well used by visitors and locals alike. Once again, the exposed beams and original stone slabs inside add to the traditional welcome that this pub offers. Here too is another opportunity to obtain good food and excellent beer.

The Dove-cote in Naunton is all that remains of a once fine Manor House that was close by. This Dove-cote, built in the 16th century has over 1000 nest-holes. Pigeon meat was very popular in those days, especially during the winter months with the wealthy landowners.

The old village pump, still to be seen on the North side of the main road through the village of Naunton.

NAUNTON to
GUITING POWER

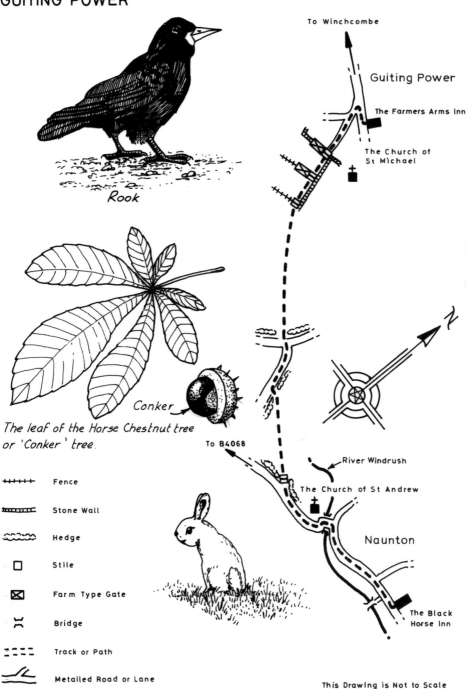

To Winchcombe

Guiting Power

The Farmers Arms Inn

The Church of
St Michael

Rook

Conker

The leaf of the Horse Chestnut tree
or 'Conker' tree.

To B4068

River Windrush

The Church of St Andrew

Naunton

The Black
Horse Inn

++++++	Fence
▦▦▦▦▦	Stone Wall
～～～	Hedge
▢	Stile
⊠	Farm Type Gate
⊃⊂	Bridge
‒ ‒ ‒ ‒	Track or Path
⌁	Metalled Road or Lane

This Drawing is Not to Scale

The Farmer's Arms Inn, Guiting Power to
The Half Way House Inn, Kineton (Distance 1½ miles)

Leave the Farmer's Arms and turn right to walk back through the village and pass the village green on your left. Look once again for the 'Wardens' Way' on your right and follow it through the cottages, out of the village and down to the River Windrush.

Where the path meets the river it divides. Leave the 'Wardens' Way' cross over the river and head left. After a short climb out of the valley, the path leads onto the Barton Road; here you turn left.

After 300 yards, after the first house on the right, turn right on a well marked footpath. Take the time to look to your left as you cross the first field. A magnificent sight awaits you, featuring the local Manor House set against the splendour of Guiting Wood.

After four fields, enter Kineton alongside the corrugated sheds of Home Farm. Turn left for the next stop at the Half Way House. This inn is truly old and once belonged to Corpus Christi College, Oxford.

Whichever season you decide to visit, you will not be disappointed. In the warm summer evenings the inn offers the use of its pleasant garden and in the winter it features real fires. Once again the menu is extensive and complemented by a range of beers.

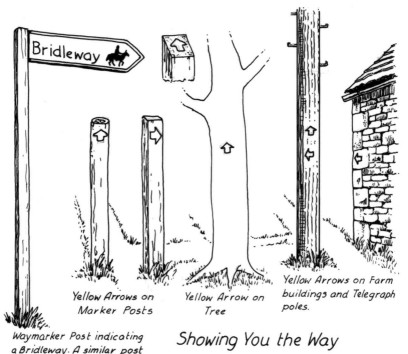

Yellow Arrows on Marker Posts

Yellow Arrow on Tree

Yellow Arrows on Farm buildings and Telegraph poles.

Waymarker Post indicating a Bridleway. A similar post indicates a Footpath.

Showing You the Way

GUITING POWER to KINETON

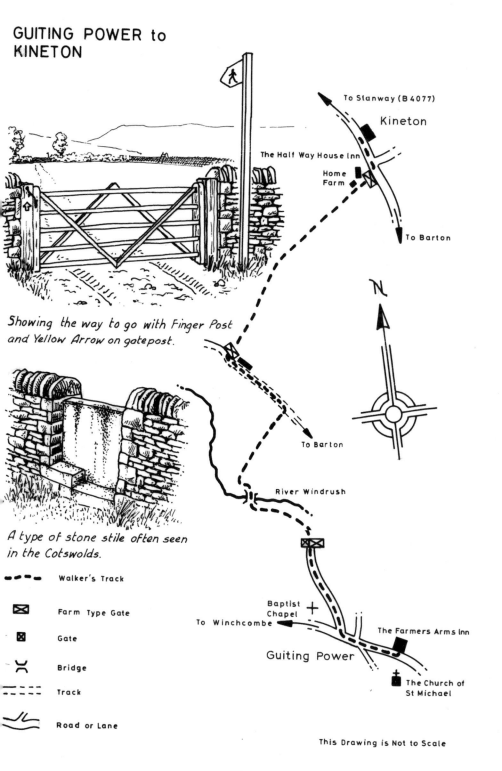

Showing the way to go with Finger Post and Yellow Arrow on gatepost.

A type of stone stile often seen in the Cotswolds.

To Stanway (B4077)

Kineton

The Half Way House Inn

Home Farm

To Barton

N

To Barton

River Windrush

Baptist Chapel

To Winchcombe

Guiting Power

The Farmers Arms Inn

The Church of St Michael

- - - - Walker's Track

⊠ Farm Type Gate

▣ Gate

⌣ Bridge

- - - - Track

⌣ Road or Lane

This Drawing is Not to Scale

The Half Way House Inn, Kineton to The Plough Inn, Ford
(Distance 2 miles)

This section starts off badly, due to the lack of an accessible footpath and a long road section to walk, but ends well.

Leave the Half Way House and turn right out of the village. Follow the unclassified road for a full mile to Temple Guiting. At the school, turn right and follow the road down into the village.

Immediately after the Manor look for a footpath sign on the left which takes you up a small lane. Here there was once the only llama farm in the Cotswolds but the llamas are long gone and the wildlife is now less exotic. The lane soon runs into a small field where you continue straight ahead. After 200 yards a footpath goes left down to the valley bottom, but ignore the signs and continue ahead.

The poorly marked footpath takes you over four fields to a small copse. Walk through the copse to join the B4077 road.

The walking now becomes potentially dangerous as you have no choice but to walk alongside the busy road for 300 yards. The next stop is found on a bend in the road, the ancient Plough Inn.

The inn is one of England's oldest and was used as a Court House in days gone by. Authentic throughout, you cannot fail to be left breathless by the sheer beauty of blackened beams set in Cotswold stone. Historical features of interest include two vast fireplaces, handmade hinges in the doors, the 'Bars up' ancient door securing device and the remains of the stocks in one bar.

The pub is particularly popular with foreign visitors, many of whom would like to take the entire building home. Once again, the Plough serves fine beers and an extensive menu renowned across the Cotswolds.

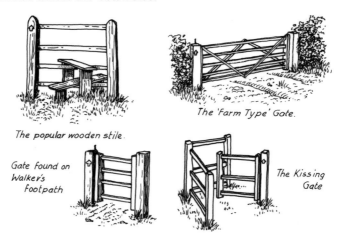

The popular wooden stile.

The 'Farm Type' Gate.

Gate found on Walker's footpath

The Kissing Gate

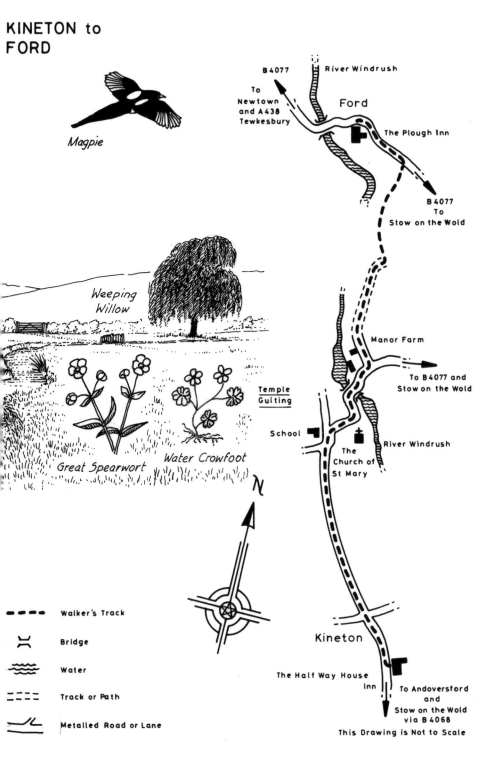

KINETON to FORD

Magpie

B 4077
To Newtown and A 438 Tewkesbury

River Windrush

Ford

The Plough Inn

B 4077 To Stow on the Wold

Weeping Willow

Manor Farm

To B 4077 and Stow on the Wold

Temple Guiting

School

River Windrush

The Church of St Mary

Great Spearwort

Water Crowfoot

N

Kineton

The Half Way House Inn

To Andoversford and Stow on the Wold via B 4068

This Drawing is Not to Scale

- - - Walker's Track

)(Bridge

≈ Water

= = = Track or Path

∿ Metalled Road or Lane

The Half Way House Inn, Kineton.

The Plough Inn, Ford.

The Snowshill Arms, Snowshill.

THE CHURCH AND POST OFFICE IN THE FAMOUS VILLAGE of SNOWSHILL IN THE COTSWOLDS OF GLOUCESTERSHIRE.

REARDON

The Plough Inn, Ford to The Snowshill Arms, Snowshill
(Distance 3 miles)

Yet another super section awaits! Leave the Plough, cross the busy B4077 and take the footpath directly opposite. After 100 yards the path divides; turn left and, after a few short steps, turn left again. After a further 250 yards the path again divides and you turn right. The path is easily followed with a series of well kept stiles and footpath markings. Very soon you emerge onto a metalled road in the hamlet of Cutsdean keeping the church on your left.

Cross the road and a small field and pick up a footpath opposite for Taddington, leaving Cutsdean alongside the old post office. Follow the path through the outbuildings of Manor Farm and, after 300 yards, turn left and walk through the valley.

Once again the footpath meets a small unclassified road, with farm buildings on your right. Turn right, ignore turnings to the left and right and follow the road for 1¼ miles to a Y junction.

At the junction there is a footpath going left into a copse. Ignore it and take a bridleway heading slightly right. It crosses three fields before once again meeting a small metalled road. Turn right and follow the road into the village of Snowshill and onto the next stop, the Snowshill Arms.

Snowshill village is a delight, built around the church and featuring an old Manor House now owned and preserved by the National Trust.

The Manor is a charming Tudor building with a 'William and Mary' front. Toys, musical instruments, spinners' and weavers' tools, clocks and bicycles pack the house from ground floor to attic and make it a treasure that should not be missed. Its pleasant, attractive terraced gardens overlook farmlands lying in the Avon Valley and Midland Plain.

Like its neighbour the Manor, the Snowshill Arms is old and retains all the qualities of a real English inn. Parts of it date back to the 13th Century and its features include exposed beams and an array of farm implements around the bar. Until the 1900s landlords brewed their own beer here. Today a range of Donnington beers are on offer to accompany a full menu of bar snacks for the hungry walker.

Snowshill

FORD to SNOWSHILL

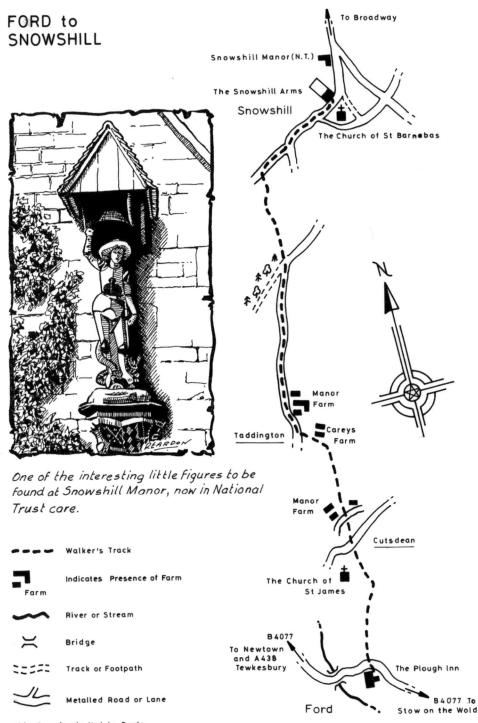

One of the interesting little figures to be found at Snowshill Manor, now in National Trust care.

To Broadway

Snowshill Manor (N.T.)

The Snowshill Arms

Snowshill

The Church of St Barnabas

N

Manor Farm

Careys Farm

Taddington

Manor Farm

Cutsdean

The Church of St James

B 4077
To Newtown
and A438
Tewkesbury

The Plough Inn

B 4077 To
Stow on the Wold

Ford

- - - - Walker's Track

▮ Farm   Indicates Presence of Farm

〜 River or Stream

╳ Bridge

▭▭▭▭ Track or Footpath

ЛL Metalled Road or Lane

This Drawing is Not to Scale

The Snowshill Arms, Snowshill to The Mount Inn, Stanton
(Distance 1¾ miles)

Keep your camera at hand as the next two sections could keep you busy. Both Snowshill and Stanton largely remain unspoilt examples of what the Cotswolds are all about and, caught in sunlight, are sights to live forever in your memory.

Leave the Snowshill Arms and make your way back out of the village in the same direction as you entered. Take the first turning right marked with a 'No Through Road' sign and very soon go right again at a Y junction. After 100 yards turn left onto a footpath. The path crosses the field at a right angle into Littleworth Wood.

Cross the stile and follow the woodland path left through the wood until once again meeting a small metalled road where you turn right.

Take care not to divert from this road as it soon crosses the 'Cotswold Way'. Continue straight ahead on what now becomes a dirt track through a metal gate.

The downhill walk offers superb panoramic views of Winchcombe, Cleeve Hill, Bredon Hill and, in the distance, the Malvern Hills. This track takes you directly to your next stop, the Mount Inn.

Again, this is a lovely unspoilt inn offering fine views from its bar and gardens.

The drawing shows an old Wellhead which at one time covered the spring – the original water supply of the Manor – which may be found in the terraced gardens of Snowshill Manor, now National Trust Property and open to the Public.

SNOWSHILL to STANTON

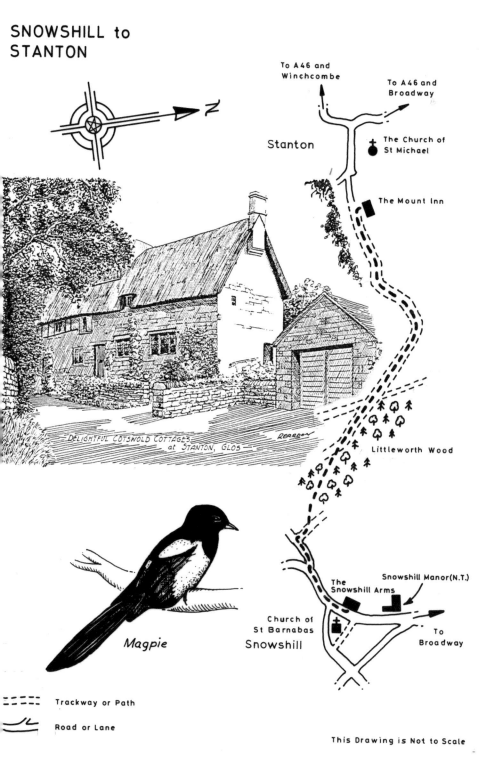

To A46 and Winchcombe

To A46 and Broadway

Stanton

The Church of St Michael

The Mount Inn

Littleworth Wood

Magpie

DELIGHTFUL COTSWOLD COTTAGES at STANTON, GLOS

REARDON

The Snowshill Arms

Snowshill Manor (N.T.)

Church of St Barnabas

Snowshill

To Broadway

- - - - Trackway or Path

Road or Lane

This Drawing is Not to Scale

The Mount Inn, Stanton to The New Inn, Willersey
(Distance 5 miles)

Stanton is one of the most picturesque villages in England, and parts of Laverton, Buckland and Broadway on your journey to Willersey could make you green with envy.

Leave the Mount and make your way down through the village. Stanton is a village of true outstanding natural beauty, which was tastefully restored by Sir Philip Stott in the early 1900s. The Jacobean House that was his home even outshines the 16th century Manor House.

At the village cross turn right for the church with its perpendicular tower and spire and its porch with two levels. It is well worth a moment of your time to go into the church and wonder at its lovingly restored interior, including two pulpits and the remains of wall paintings in the north transept.

The way now follows a well marked footpath which goes through the churchyard and runs around to the right of the church. As you leave the churchyard the path divides; turn left and, after 300 yards, go through a kissing gate and turn right for Laverton.

You are soon walking parallel with the main road but would hardly know it as it seems you are in the heart of the countryside. After four fields you join a metalled road; turn right to loop around Laverton.

The route takes you past tastefully renovated cottages and a small village green. Opposite is a 'telephone kiosk' sign alongside a bridleway. Take the bridleway which soon takes you to Buckland.

This is a delightful village with a fascinating church containing 15th century glass and 17th century seating and pulpit. Buckland Rectory is one of the oldest medieval parsonages in the country and dates back to the 15th Century.

On entering Buckland, turn right and walk up the sparsely built main road and past picture postcard houses and the Buckland Manor Hotel.

Follow the road past Buckland Court on your right. Here the barns and outbuildings have been tastefully converted into holiday accommodation. As the road climbs right look for a footpath sign in the left hand corner of 'Hillside Cottage' and 'The Bothy'.

After 50 yards the path divides and you turn left. The footpath is well marked but should be followed on your map. It takes you around the wood, steadily climbing before entering a second wood and ending at a stile. Cross the stile and walk downhill to join the 'Cotswold Way' at a minor road. Follow the 'Cotswold Way' across the fields into the tourist haunt of Broadway.

Wide streets, bordered with trim greens, and 17th and 18th century houses make up Broadway which is, without doubt, one of England's show villages.

STANTON to WILLERSEY

Broadway retains a high degree of charm and beauty and offers a number of interesting shops and tea rooms.

Walk through the main street and eventually turn left on the B4632 Leamington Road. Take the last estate road on your right into Sandscroft Avenue and follow the estate round for about 300 yards. Alongside number 35 is a footpath which twists its way across several fields (and a busy by-pass which should be crossed with care) before emerging on the driveway for Warners Farm. Turn left down the driveway onto the B4632 then turn right.

The road takes you directly into Willersey and your next stop, the New Inn. Once again, in the tradition of Donnington Inns, the New Inn has its origins stretching back more than 300 to 400 years. A range of pub games are on offer as well as good food and excellent beer.

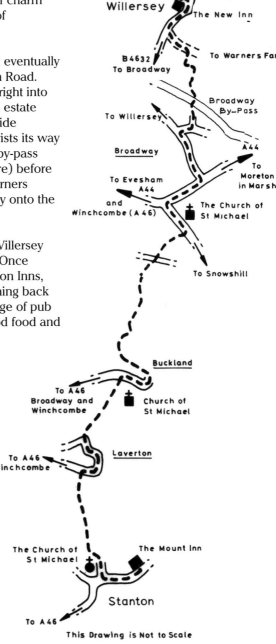

Walker's Track

Driveway or Track

Road or Lane

The New Inn, Willersey to The Black Bear Inn, Moreton-in-Marsh (Distance 9¼ miles)

The route between Willersey and Moreton-in-Marsh takes in yet more Cotswold treasures, including Chipping Campden, Broad Campden and Blockley.

Leave the New Inn and walk along the B4632 to arguably one of the finest village ponds in England. Turn right into Church Street and make your way to St. Peter's church. Here you pick up a footpath running left through the churchyard and, where the path divides, take the right hand path. Cross the stream on a stone bridge and take the left hand path. Cross a second stream almost immediately and keep to the right. After 50 yards, turn right and head for the church with a very pointed spire on the hill. This is St. Nicholas's church at Saintbury and well worth a visit, containing as it does a 15th century font and 18th century cover, looking over equally old box pews.

From the lower churchyard gate, walk down towards the village. Where the lane joins a road, turn right and walk up the road for about 20 yards before taking a footpath on your left. Follow the yellow arrowed route. After a pleasant walk, the path crosses a bridleway. Ignore the bridleway signs and continue straight ahead on the footpath.

After 30 yards, cross the stream on a wooden bridge. At this point the path divides three ways; continue straight ahead and climb the hill. The path eventually comes out onto a minor road; here you turn right and follow the road uphill.

After a short distance, at a National Trust sign for Dover's Hill, turn left through a kissing gate and climb to the right to a topograph. Here is a magnificent view of the surrounding countryside.

Dover's Hill is the site of the famous Cotswold Games, founded during the reign of James I by Captain Robert Dover. They continue today, although their history is chequered due to their suppression during the Cromwellian period and, in later years, the behaviour of riotous Irish navvies in 1851 who, no doubt, would have revelled in the favourite Cotswold 'game' of shin-kicking.

Continue to your right around the escarpment to a trig point. Just past the trig point turn right onto a well used track that takes you down to Chipping Campden. Your walk into this lovely town may well whet your appetite to next walk the 'Cotswold Way' a fine, long distance walk which starts here.

Chipping Campden is arguably the finest of the Cotswold wool towns and was at the height of its prosperity in the late Middle Ages. It has aged with grace and, while catering for the tourist, has not lowered its standards to pander to them.

At St. Catherine's church turn left and then first right into Sheep Street. The route you are about to take leads you out of Chipping Campden but a diversion into the town is well worth taking. Of the many architectural delights on offer, there are gems in the form of Grevel's House, Bedfont House and the charming little Woolstaplers' Hall Museum.

WILLERSEY to MORETON in MARSH

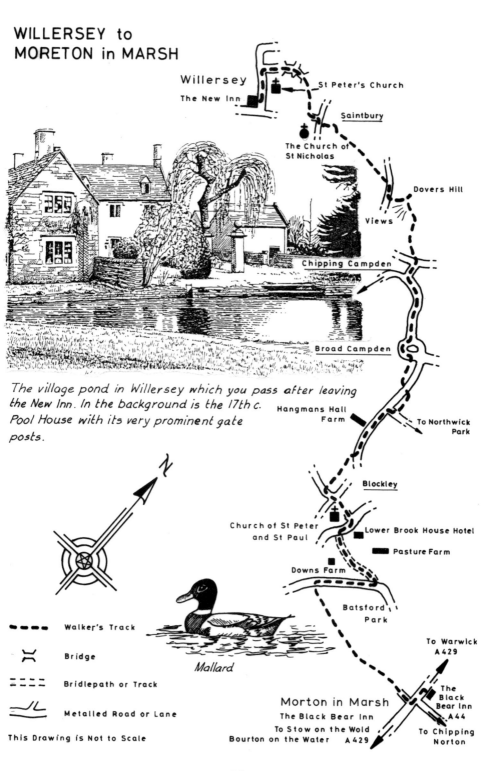

Willersey

The New Inn

St Peter's Church

Saintbury

The Church of St Nicholas

Dovers Hill

Views

Chipping Campden

Broad Campden

The village pond in Willersey which you pass after leaving the New Inn. In the background is the 17th c. Pool House with its very prominent gate posts.

Hangmans Hall Farm

To Northwick Park

Blockley

Church of St Peter and St Paul

Lower Brook House Hotel

Pasture Farm

Downs Farm

Batsford Park

N

Mallard

— — — Walker's Track

⋈ Bridge

= = = = Bridlepath or Track

↶↷ Metalled Road or Lane

This Drawing is Not to Scale

To Warwick A 429

The Black Bear Inn A 44

Morton in Marsh

The Black Bear Inn

To Stow on the Wold

Bourton on the Water A 429

To Chipping Norton

35

After 300 yards of Sheep Street, turn left on an unclassified road to Broad Campden. Wind your way carefully through this affluent village and climb a small rise of the road. Just past a house named 'The Farthings' turn right onto a public footpath. This climbs steeply up a rough field before rejoining the unclassified road to Blockley. Cross straight over and turn right in the woods on a path which runs parallel to the road.

When the path meets an estate road, turn right and rejoin the road, then turn left. Approximately 300 yards past Hangman's Hall Farm, as the road sweeps left, turn right and climb up a well marked bridleway. At the top of the rise, the bridleway doubles back to the right; however you go left on a yellow arrowed footpath soon dropping into the valley floor.

A steady climb uphill eventually brings you to a flatter, grassy area. Walk to the right hand field boundary to find an unmarked path which runs straight ahead across a field and into the houses of Blockley. Turn left down Greenway Road and right into Park Road.

Blockley is a mysterious village with steep streets of character terraces, full of 17th, 18th and 19th century buildings. Owing much of its prosperity to the silk trade, Blockley once boasted six mills employing more than 500 people.

Turn left into the parish churchyard and take time out to visit the church which was the first in England to be lit by electricity. Go left again in front of the church, drop down to the B4479 road and turn right.

Just past Lower Brook House, turn left on a bridleway marked 'Pasture Farm'. At the top of the rise take the blue arrowed bridleway to the right of a large barn. Follow the bridleway around the escarpment until it divides several ways.

Turn right on a poorly marked path, keeping Downs Farm on your right. Cross a ladder stile and continue right to a small unclassified road. Join the road and again turn right.

You now have a large estate wall on your left. After approximately a quarter of a mile, the wall goes left and you follow it on a well used footpath around the estate and downhill, to eventually pass two gatehouses on your left hand side.

The well signed path crosses several fields before emerging in Moreton-in-Marsh. On reaching the houses, walk straight ahead for the Market Place and the next stop, the Black Bear Inn. This is reputed to be haunted by a ghost called 'Fred' who has been known to play tricks on customers.

The large inn offers accommodation, good food and of course yet another chance to sample a wide range of Donnington ales.

The Mount Inn, Stanton.

The New Inn, Willersey

The Black Bear Inn, Moreton-in-Marsh to The Red Lion Inn, Little Compton (Distance 5¼ miles)

Leave the Black Bear and take the busy A44 out of Moreton-in-Marsh for a full one and a half miles until you pass the Fire Service College. Take the unclassified road left, marked Great Wolford, at the Four Shires Stone.

The stone is an impressive 18th century monument topped by a sundial and a ball, marking the old boundaries of the counties of Gloucestershire, Warwickshire, Oxfordshire and Worcestershire. (NB. The Worcestershire section has long been swallowed up into Gloucestershire.)

Walk up the road for one third of a mile to a burial plot and turn right into a field on a footpath marked 'Seven Shires Way'. You now cross several fields on a poorly signed path until you arrive at a deer fence with a gate in it. Go through the gate and straight ahead through the break in the trees, then through another three deer fence gates. Now aim for the left side of the Manor House again on a poorly marked path. When you eventually join a dirt track, turn right into Barton-on-the-Heath. This village was once the home of Captain Robert Dover (mentioned earlier), the 17th century lawyer and founder of the 'Cotswold Games'.

At the road junction turn right, marked 'Little Compton'. Stay on this road through the village and past St. Lawrence's church. Approximately 100 yards after the church turn left onto a marked footpath and follow arrowed direction signs for the next one and a half miles.

Head for Salters Well Farm. At the farm pass the farmhouse on your right, go through a gate, turn left, ignore the bridleway sign and, after a few short steps, turn right to follow the footpath downhill. At the bottom of the hill turn right and then left on a footpath leading to your next port of call, the Red Lion in Little Compton, Warwickshire's most southerly village.

The inn was built in the 16th Century and boasts a fine lounge/restaurant and an exceptionally pretty garden. The Red Lion serves good meals and a fine selection of Donnington ales.

The Duck Pond
Moreton in Marsh

MORETON in MARSH to
LITTLE COMPTON

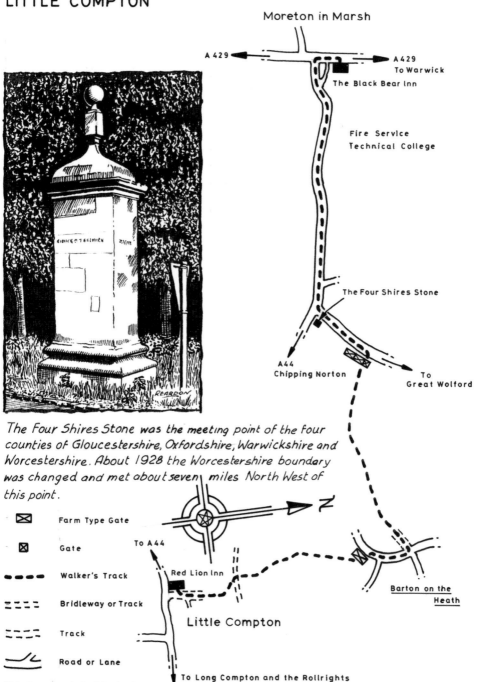

Moreton in Marsh

A 429

A 429
To Warwick

The Black Bear Inn

Fire Service
Technical College

The Four Shires Stone

A44
Chipping Norton

To
Great Wolford

The Four Shires Stone was the meeting point of the four
counties of Gloucestershire, Oxfordshire, Warwickshire and
Worcestershire. About 1928 the Worcestershire boundary
was changed and met about seven miles North West of
this point.

To A44

Red Lion Inn

Barton on the
Heath

Little Compton

To Long Compton and the Rollrights

	Farm Type Gate
	Gate
●●●●	Walker's Track
= = = =	Bridleway or Track
= = = =	Track
⌣⌐	Road or Lane

This Drawing is Not to Scale

The Red Lion Inn, Little Compton to The Fox Inn, Broadwell
(Distance 4½ miles)

This section proved to be the most difficult to piece together without resorting to roads to join the villages of Evenlode and Broadwell. However, the effort is rewarded as you will find Broadwell to be a delight.

Leave the Red Lion and cross over the road behind the car park. Look to your left and you will find a well signed footpath taking you around a small field to the busy A44 road. Cross straight over and join an unclassified road to Chastleton.

After a quarter of a mile, turn left into a field on a footpath which eventually takes you over three fields to emerge alongside Chastleton church and its magnificent Manor House. It was built for a local wool merchant, Walter Jones and is now owned and maintained by the National Trust.

Turn left at the church and follow the road uphill for a quarter of a mile. When the road sweeps right and then left, leave it and go in to Peasewell Wood. The way divides. Turn right onto the bridleway which can get very muddy. Continue straight ahead, ignoring turnings to your left, for some distance, to drop down to Horn Farm. Join a metalled road taking you into Evenlode.

At the road junction turn left. Unfortunately, there is no alternative now but to use roads for the next one and a half miles. Follow the minor roads which take you left out of Evenlode and then right towards Broadwell. The road leads you straight into the heart of the village. At the end of Chapel Street turn right for the village green and your next stop, the Fox Inn.

Broadwell is a spacious village whose church stands in a tree-shaded churchyard and features several dignified 17th century table tombs. Here too is a monument dedicated to Herbert Weston and his wife, kneeling at a prayer desk.

The Fox is traditionally built in Cotswold stone, facing the spacious green which itself is a popular venue for picnickers and touring groups of Morris Men. Inside is a real 'village' atmosphere. The inn offers an extensive menu and a range of Donnington beers. This is the fifteenth and final inn on your walk. However, to get back to your starting point and complete the circle you now have a second opportunity to visit the Queen's Head at Stow-on-the-Wold.

The 'Farm Type' Gate.

40

LITTLE COMPTON to BROADWELL

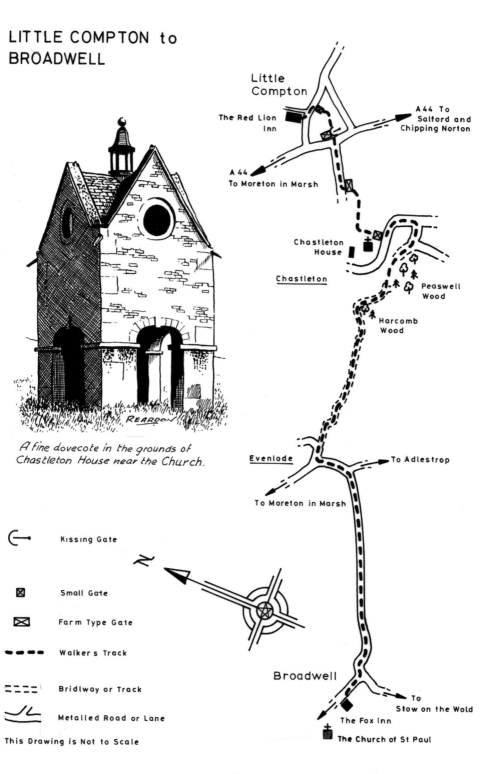

A fine dovecote in the grounds of Chastleton House near the Church.

Little Compton

The Red Lion Inn

A44 To Salford and Chipping Norton

A44 To Moreton in Marsh

Chastleton House

Chastleton

Peaswell Wood

Harcomb Wood

Evenlode

To Adlestrop

To Moreton in Marsh

Broadwell

To Stow on the Wold

The Fox Inn

The Church of St Paul

Kissing Gate

Small Gate

Farm Type Gate

Walkers Track

Bridlway or Track

Metalled Road or Lane

This Drawing is Not to Scale

The Fox Inn, Broadwell to The Queen's Head Inn, Stow-on-the-Wold
(Distance 1½ miles)

From the Fox Inn, walk back down the green and turn right on the road to Stow-on-the-Wold. Follow the road uphill and, after about a quarter of a mile, turn left on a well marked and well used bridleway which takes you directly into Stow-on-the-Wold and the Queen's Head.

The old Stocks on the Green in the Square in Stow on the Wold.

The famous old well known as "The Wells". Believed to be about 2000 years old, the water from the spring is crystal clear.

BROADWELL to
STOW on the WOLD

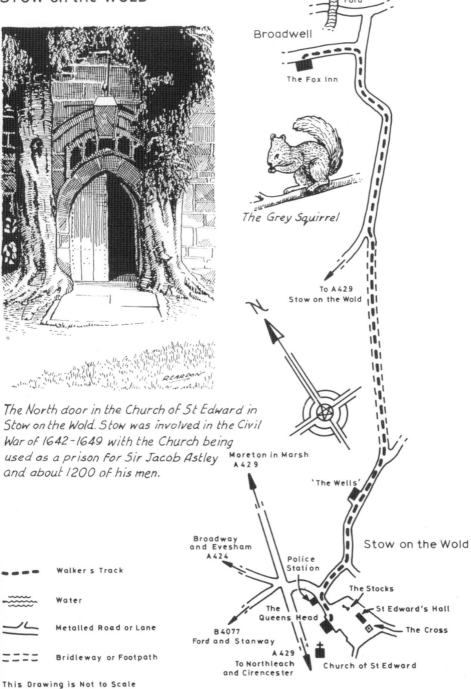

Ford

Broadwell

The Fox Inn

The Grey Squirrel

To A429
Stow on the Wold

N

The North door in the Church of St Edward in
Stow on the Wold. Stow was involved in the Civil
War of 1642-1649 with the Church being
used as a prison for Sir Jacob Astley
and about 1200 of his men.

Moreton in Marsh
A429

'The Wells'

Broadway
and Evesham
A424

Police
Station

Stow on the Wold

The Stocks

St Edward's Hall

The
Queens Head

The Cross

B4077
Ford and Stanway

A429
To Northleach
and Cirencester

Church of St Edward

- - - - - Walker s Track

~~~~~ Water

⌐⌐ Metalled Road or Lane

= = = = Bridleway or Footpath

This Drawing is Not to Scale

43

The Red Lion, Little Compton.

The Fox Inn, Broadwell.